D1614108

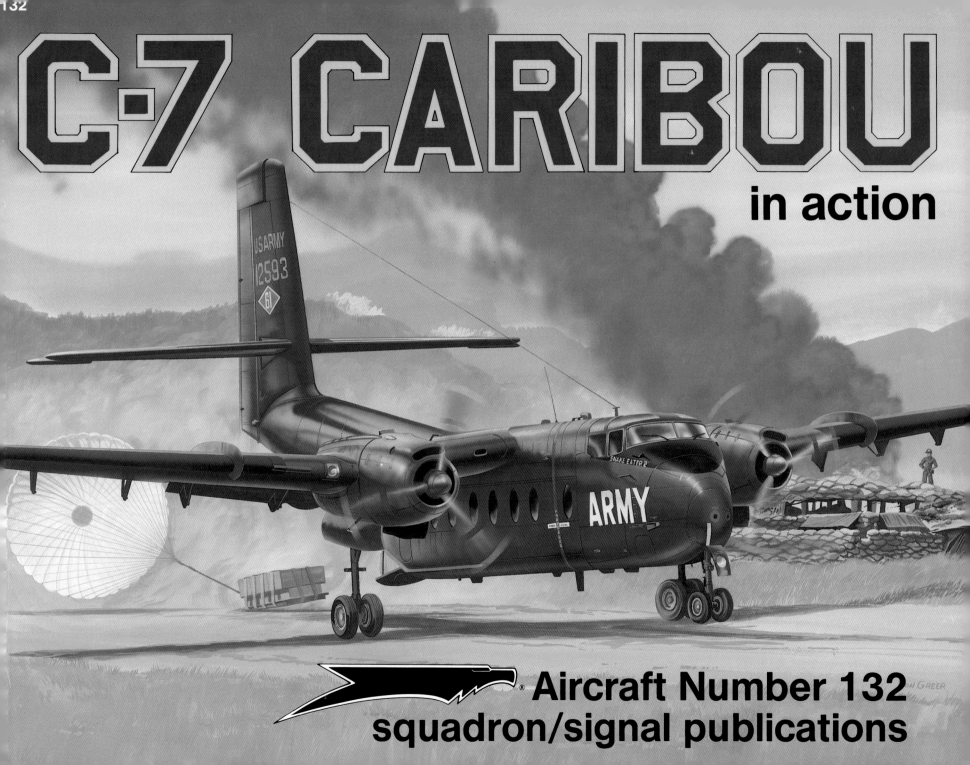

C-7 CARIBOU

in action

US ARMY
12593
61

SNAKE EATER 2

ARMY

Aircraft Number 132

squadron/signal publications

C-7 CARIBOU

in action

by Wayne Mutza

Color by Don Greer & Tom Tullis
Illustrated by Joe Sewell

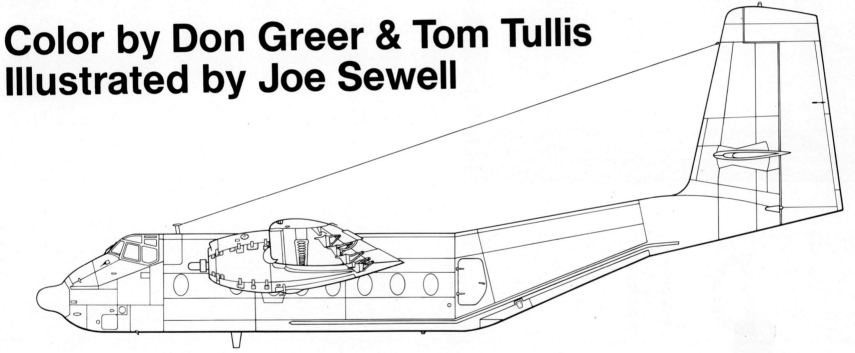

Aircraft Number 132
squadron/signal publications

Snake Eater 2, a CV-2A Caribou of the 61st Aviation Company, skims the runway as it makes a Low Level Extraction System supply drop to a remote outpost near Ban Me Thuot, South Vietnam during the early 1960s.

ISBN 0-89747-292-6

If you have any photographs of the aircraft, armor, soldiers or ships of any nation, particularly wartime snapshots, why not share them with us and help make Squadron/Signal's books all the more interesting and complete in the future. Any photograph sent to us will be copied and the original returned. The donor will be fully credited for any photos used. Please send them to:

Squadron/Signal Publications, Inc.
1115 Crowley Drive.
Carrollton, TX 75011-5010.

Dedication

This book is respectfully dedicated to Deb and to all who had the distinction of serving with the "Bou." They, like the aircraft they flew and maintained, deserve recognition for their exemplary service.

Acknowledgements

Al Adcock
Terry Love
Norm Taylor
U.S. Army
Chas. Van Hulsentop

Tom Hansen
Bob Pickett
Geoff Tierney
U.S. Air Force
Al Drake

Army Otter and Caribou Association
Jack Calve - US Army Avn Systems Command
Sharon Condotta - DeHavilland

A flight of AC-1 Caribous of the 1st Aviation Company taxi out for another mission from Korat, Thailand. The aircraft are finished in overall Gloss Olive Drab with high visibility markings. The Army logo and serial on the fin was in Yellow.

3

Introduction

During the 1950s, the U.S. Army began to aggressively develop its support aviation branch and began a long association with aircraft built by DeHavilland of Canada (DHC). Previously restricted to small reconnaissance aircraft, the Army had won the right to purchase Short Take-Off and Landing (STOL) aircraft and chose DeHavilland of Canada (DHC) through open competition, despite strong opposition from the U.S. aviation industry which opposed any purchase of foreign built aircraft for use by U.S. forces. The first DHC aircraft used by the Army was the DHC-2 Beaver. The Beaver joined the Army during 1951 under the designation L-20 and was followed by its larger brother, the DHC-3 (U-1) Otter during 1955.

Since DHC's design concepts for arctic and bush aircraft meshed closely with Army requirements, a close bond was formed between the company and the Army. As the Army expanded their STOL air arm, the U.S. Air Force began taking a dim view of the growing Army air branch, since there were many in the Air Force that felt their area of responsibility (and funding) were being infringed upon. When the Army announced its intent to team a new STOL transport with the Boeing Vertol CH-47 helicopter to perform its front line medium transport mission and replace their fleet of aging reciprocal powered helicopters, the stage was set for an inter-service power struggle. The Army hoped that the new team of fixed wing transport and large support helicopter would further define their evolving theory of air mobility.

The Army requirement for the new transport combined the load-carrying capacity of the Douglas DC-3/C-47 with the proven STOL performance of the Beaver and Otter. With the Army requirement in mind, DHC began design work on the DHC-4 during 1954. The aircraft was envisioned as an enlarged twin-engined Otter with fixed landing gear, a rear loading ramp and a gross weight of 13,000 pounds. This design was scrapped on the drawing board as the Army requirement was refined. The new requirement called for a rugged STOL three ton tactical transport with rear loading and the same load carrying capability as the CH-47.

During the design process, DHC considered two types of tail configuration: a twin fin and a single vertical tail. The latter was chosen along with a retractable landing gear. A good deal of attention was given to cabin size and cargo loading since the Army insisted on an adjustable rear loading ramp and inward folding doors. To give the aircraft good STOL capability, large double-slotted flaps spanned the entire wing, similar to those on the Otter.

Five power plants were studied before DeHavilland decided on the proven Pratt & Whitney 1,450 hp R-2000 series of air cooled radial engines. The use of these engines allowed a maximum weight of 28,500 pounds. Turbine engines were ruled out at this stage but would figure into a later design, the DHC-5 Buffalo.

In a hurry to get their new transports, the Army purchased the design off the drawing board on the basis of preliminary drawings and specifications. The Pentagon ordered five preproduction evaluation aircraft during early 1957 under the designation YAC-1 Caribou. At a maximum gross weight of 26,000 pounds, the Caribou became the heaviest fixed-wing aircraft used by the Army (except for six P-2 Neptunes acquired on a loan basis from the Navy for special purposes in 1966). Because of the compressed development time table, wind tunnel models were used to establish airfoil properties through a unique set of tests. A fully instrumented model was mounted on the front of a truck and driven up and down the runway. A year later, a similar scale model was mounted on a framework carried on the back of a DHC-3 Otter to provide a quick source of aerodynamic test data.

An instrumented scale model of the Caribou prototype was mounted on a frame carried over the fuselage of a DHC-3 Otter during 1957 to gather aerodynamic test data. (DeHavilland)

A trio of engineers go over details of the first Caribou prototype during the early stages of its construction at the DeHavilland facility. The second prototype was also under construction in the background. (DeHavilland)

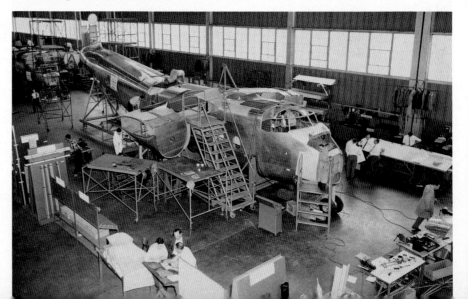

Following an all-out effort, the first DHC-4 prototype (Caribou number one) made its maiden test flight on 30 July 1958 and underwent extensive tests registered as CF-KTK-X until delivery to the Canadian government on 5 September 1959. The prototype was a large aircraft weighing in at a gross weight of 26,000 pounds. The prototype was initially fitted with Pratt & Whitney R-2000D-5 engines but, in early 1961, it underwent extensive modifications to the wings and was used as a test bed for the General Electric T-64 turbine engines intended for the Caribou II (DHC-5 Buffalo), making its first flight on 22 September 1961. When testing was completed it was converted back to standard configuration. The second prototype built, CF-LAX-X, also went to the Canadian government and was later leased to Nordair in 1961 for rough arctic field tests.

Technicians and DHC officials inspect the first Caribou prototype following its official rollout in July of 1958. The open hatch above the cockpit is the upper fuselage emergency escape hatch. (DeHavilland)

The first prototype was extensively modified during 1961 to serve as a test bed for the General Electric GE T-64 turboprop engines, later used in the DHC-5 Buffalo. (DeHavilland)

The Caribou prototype, DHC-4 number one, takes off on its maiden flight on 30 July 1958 with an instrument test probe fitted to the nose. At this point, the landing gear doors had not been installed. (DeHavilland)

5

Development

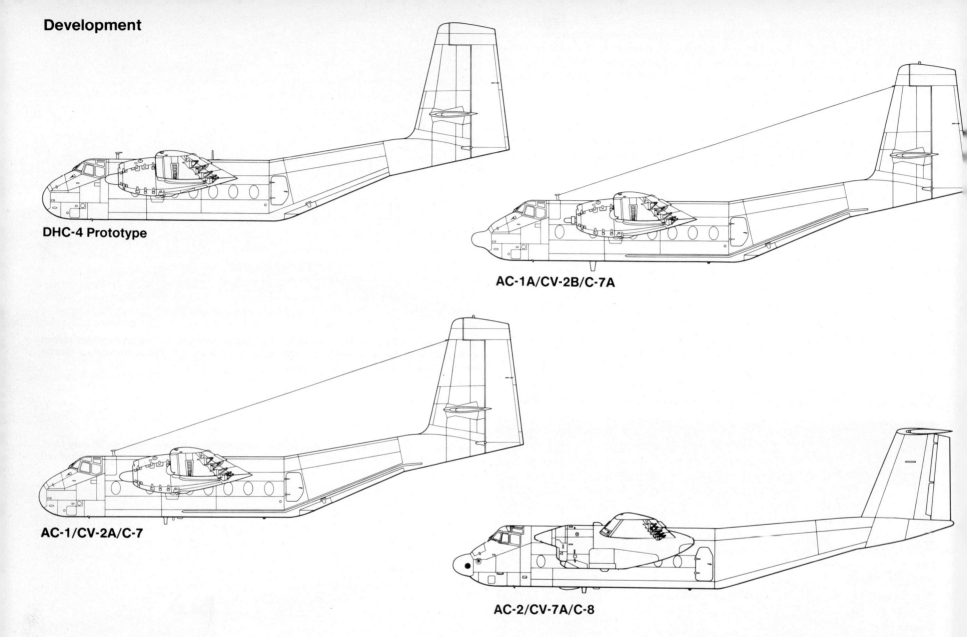

DHC-4 Prototype

AC-1A/CV-2B/C-7A

AC-1/CV-2A/C-7

AC-2/CV-7A/C-8

YAC-1 Caribou

The two prototypes were followed on the assembly line by the five pre-production YAC-1 service test aircraft which had been ordered by the U.S. Army during 1957. The YAC-1 (57-3079) flew for the first time in March of 1959, but was lost on a test flight after developing tail flutter (on 24 February 1959). Investigation revealed that the crash stemmed from a design flaw in a fuselage modification which had added forty-five inches to the overall fuselage length. This modification had been done to establish a broader center of gravity range for the aircraft. The flutter problem was fixed by stiffening the control cable systems. Another problem that was discovered with the first YAC-1 was a tendency to yaw. This was caused by a vortex coming off the rear fuselage rounded edges. A dorsal fin was added to the vertical fin to correct the problem but this modification proved ineffective. Strakes were then added along the lower fuselage sides which finally corrected the problem.

To increase STOL performance, the second YAC-1 (s/n 57-3080) was modified with drooped wing leading edges and fitted with wing fences, stall bars and stall warning devices (which became standard on all later Caribous). The first three YAC-1s were delivered to the Army on 8 October 1958 followed by the remaining two which were handed over in November. The fourth YAC-1 (s/n 57-3082) was used to test an autopilot, reversing propellers and wing and tail leading edge de-icers (which became standard on production Caribous). The fifth prototype (57-3079) replaced the crashed aircraft. All early Caribous featured three-section main landing gear doors and the last three YAC-1s were fitted with a forward under fuselage fairing which housed test instruments.

The YAC-1s were powered by two 1,450 hp Pratt & Whitney fourteen cylinder two-row radial air cooled engines driving Hamilton Standard three-blade full-feathering constant-speed propellers. The exhaust system on the YAC-1 differed from the DHC-4 prototype in that the over wing exhaust stacks were nearly twice as long as the stacks used on the prototype. At sea level the Caribou has a cruising speed of 170 mph. At 7,500 feet, using only 50% of its available power, it could cruise at 182 mph, giving it a range of 1,400 miles.

The cranked fuselage and immense vertical tail surfaces were the dominant features. The upswept rear fuselage provided access to the rear cargo door and the clearance under the tail permitted truck loading. The lower position of the rear door served as an adjustable ramp and ramp extensions were provided for vehicle loading. The upward folding door formed the fuselage underside. Both doors could be opened in flight for paradropping troops or supplies. The fuselage belly comprised three heavily supported longitudinal beams which kept damage from wheels-up landings to a minimum. The massive tail surfaces were necessary to provide adequate stability and control at low speeds.

The wing featured full span double-slotted flaps, with the outboard trailing sections also serving as ailerons. This arrangement provided excellent control and maneuverability, especially during low level, low speed operations. A marked wing anhedral lowered the thrust line, reduced the length of the main landing gear, and improved the pilot's rear vision.

The wide center of gravity range allowed a broad variety of cargo to be carried. The cabin could accommodate either thirty-two combat troops (in wall mounted folding seats), twenty-four paratroops, twenty-two stretchers, two jeeps or three tons of cargo. The cabin was twenty-nine feet in length, over six feet high and just over seven feet wide. Overall the Caribou was seventy-two feet seven inches long and thirty-one feet nine inches high with a wing span of ninety-five feet seven and one half inches.

The Caribou's high absorption rugged landing gear was a tricycle type with dual wheels on all units. The main gear retracted forward while the hydraulically steerable nose gear retracted rearward. Ski landing gear could be installed within two and a half hours without the use of jacks or special equipment.

Fuel capacity for the Caribou was 828 gallons carried in ten-cell wing tanks outboard of both engines. The cockpit offered excellent all-around visibility for the crew which comprised a pilot, copilot, and crew chief or flight engineer. All radio equipment was located on a console between the pilot's seats which, when not in use, slid forward on runners into the instrument panel. The fuselage had two rear entrance doors, a jettisonable hatch below the cockpit, a roof hatch over the cockpit and an emergency hatch in the port cabin wall to the rear of the cockpit.

Following the prototype crash in 1959, and with no new orders coming in, DHC decided that a worldwide sales trip was necessary to make the Caribou project viable. DeHavilland's world demonstration tour was flown by the ninth and final pre-production aircraft (CF-LVA) beginning in October of 1959. The tour, which covered 40 countries and accomplished 479 demonstrations flights in 221 days over 50,000 miles, was very successful and prompted sales from some of the largest Caribou customers.

The fourth pre-production YAC-1 (57-3082) was the first to be fitted with fuselage strakes and was also the first to be fitted with a leading edge deicer system. At this point in the flight test program, the aircraft still carried its civil registration on the tail. (DeHavilland)

7

The YAC-1 Caribou passed its first field test with flying colors. The U.S. Army's 1st Aviation Company operated their YAC-1s under simulated combat conditions for some six weeks during mid-1961. During this intensive shake-down, they flew from rough fields and clearings that were less than 2,000 feet in length. They flew in bad weather, day and night, often hauling full loads of troops and equipment, including Hawk and Honest John missiles. The five preproduction YAC-1s were never brought up to production Caribou standards and available records indicate that the YAC-1s remained in the Army inventory throughout their operational lives.

Following the crash in 1974 of the C-47 used by the U.S. Army's Golden Knights Parachute Demonstration Team, the first YAC-1 Caribou (57-3079) became the team jump ship. This task was later accomplished by two of the other YAC-1s (3082 and 3083) well into the 1980s. With more than 6,000 flying hours on her airframe, 3082 ended its long flying life in August of 1986 and was later donated to the airlift museum at Pope AFB, NC. The second YAC-1 (3080) supported the Army's Silver Eagles Flight Demonstration Team during the late 1970s and ended its career in late 1983 when it was put to rest at the Army Aviation Museum at Fort Rucker, AL.

The third YAC-1, on the ramp at the Wichita Municipal Airport in December of 1972, was repainted in an overall White paint scheme with Red/Orange wing and tail panels for arctic tests. The Black nose radome was a retrofit and belly instrument fairing was also in Black. (J.P. Loomis via Bob Pickett)

YAC-1 Development

DHC-4 Prototype

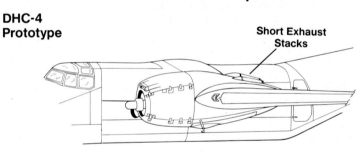

Short Exhaust Stacks

The five YAC-1s were finished at the factory in overall Gloss Olive Drab with Yellow serials on the fin and a White Army logo on the nose. This YAC-1, conducting a short-field takeoff demonstration at Fort Rucker, AL in October of 1960, was the third YAC-1 built. (U.S. Army)

YAC-1

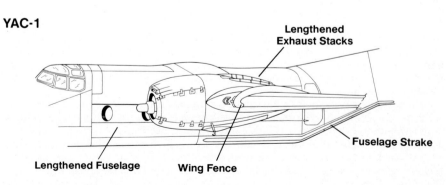

Lengthened Exhaust Stacks

Fuselage Strake

Lengthened Fuselage   Wing Fence

While assigned to the Aviation Board during mid-1961 for tests, the fourth YAC-1 was finished in an Arctic paint scheme and outfitted with ski landing gear. The narrow belly instrument fairing was installed on the last three YAC-1s. (DeHavilland)

The cockpit had a practical arrangement with excellent pilot visibility. The radio console in the center slid forward into the instrument panel when not in use. The foot pedals incorporated both brakes and rudder control with the brakes at the top while the lower half were the rudder pedals. (DeHavilland)

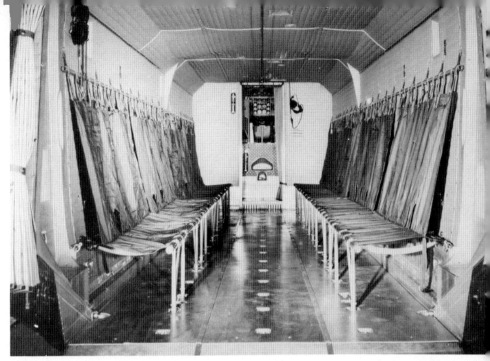

With troop seats folded down, the cargo cabin could accommodate thirty-two combat troops. Once operational, Caribous were often flown without the luxury of the all-around sound-proofing installed in this early YAC-1. When not in use, the seats folded up along the fuselage side. (Smithsonian Institution)

The final YAC-1 Caribou (3083) on a test flight shortly after it was delivered to the Army in November of 1958. The preproduction YAC-1 aircraft remained in the Army inventory for their entire service lives. (Smithsonian Institution)

9

The final YAC-1 (3083) was assigned to the Transportation Test and Support Activity (TATSA) in December of 1959 and carried that command's logo on the fuselage side. During Project MAN (early May of 1960) the aircraft was based at Lawson Army Air Field, Fort Benning, Ga. (U.S. Army)

Registered CF-LAN, the second pre-production Caribou went to the Canadian government. For a while it served as a demonstrator conducting several demonstrations at Fort Eustis, VA. The aircraft was leased to Nordair during 1961 and was later acquired by Air America. At last report, it was flying for the Environmental Research Institution of Michigan. (U.S. Army)

During late 1975, the fourth YAC-1 was assigned to the Golden Knights parachute team. In this role the aircraft carried a paint scheme of Gloss White over Gloss Olive Drab with Day-Glo Orange wing and tail panels. The aircraft was later donated to the airlift museum at Pope AFB, NC in September of 1986. (Bob Pickett)

The fourth YAC-1 was surrounded by support equipment during routine maintenance at New Cumberland Army Depot during 1964. On the fuselage just behind the cockpit was painted a Blue bird with the USA above it and RSG below it. (Al Adcock)

The second YAC-1 served as the support aircraft for the Army Silver Eagles Helicopter Demonstration Team from 1976 to 1979 during which time it carried a Gloss White over Gloss Dark Blue paint scheme. The aircraft now rests at the aviation museum, Fort Rucker, AL. (Hugh Muir via Terry Love)

Resplendent in its Gloss White and Gloss Black show scheme, the first YAC-1 was used as a jump aircraft by the Army's Golden Knights Parachute Demonstration team during the 1970s. (Norm Taylor)

The third prototype ended its long Army career at the Davis-Monthan Air Force Base storage facility. The aircraft was destroyed by a wind storm during 1985. (Terry Love)

11

AC-1/CV-2A

The Army placed an initial order for seven production aircraft under the designation AC-1 during early 1960 with the first aircraft (60-3762) being delivered during January of 1961. The second AC-1 was delivered to the Army Aviation Test Board on 3 April 1961 and the third example was modified to include an Aerial Delivery Kit prior to delivery.

Production Caribous were powered by two 1,450 hp Pratt & Whitney R2000-7MD air cooled radial engines housed in a three section "petal" cowling. The cowling consisted of three main sections which opened much like the petals of a flower to ease maintenance. For engine changes or other major work, each section was completely detachable. The R2000-7MD gave the AC-1 a maximum speed of 216 mph at a gross weight of 26,000 pounds (empty weight was 17,630 pounds). Cruising speed at 10,000 feet was 182 mph and the rate of climb at sea level was 1,355 feet per minute. Fully loaded, the Caribou had an impressive stall speed of 65 mph. On a short field takeoff the AC-1, at max gross weight, could get off the ground in 540 feet. For obstacle takeoffs, the AC-1 could clear a 50 foot obstacle after a 1,020 foot run. Short field landings could be accomplished within 525 feet or 1,235 feet over a 50 foot obstacle. Service ceiling on two engines was 24,800 feet and 8,800 feet on one engine. Carrying a 5,400 pound payload, the Caribou had a range of 1,100 miles (at 150 mph). This gave the aircraft a maximum endurance of seven and a half hours and a maximum range of 1,400 miles.

The production Caribou differed from the prototypes in a number of ways (although none significantly altered the Caribou's basic airframe). The only modification which actually improved the aircraft's performance was the relocation of the fuel tank fillers to the top of the wing, which allowed the tanks to be more fully utilized and increased the fuel capacity from 720 to 828 gallons.

The prototype's three-section main landing gear doors were changed to a two section gear door on the production AC-1 and the right cabin passenger door was made jettisonable. The auxiliary power unit (APU) was relocated from the left engine nacelle to the left

The first production AC-1 (60-3762) prepares to touch down at an Army Air Field during early 1961. The U.S. Army and serial number on the fin were in Yellow while the ARMY logo on the nose was in White. (U.S. Army)

fuselage side. An oxygen system was installed and web seats were installed in the cabin replacing the earlier solid seats.

A total of fifty-six AC-1s were built by June of 1961. These aircraft were redesignated in 1962 to CV-2A and when the aircraft were transferred to the Air Force they were again redesignated, becoming C-7s.

Main Landing Gear Doors

YAC-1

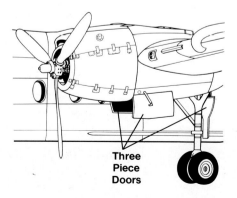

Three Piece Doors

AC-1

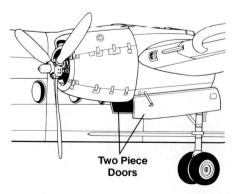

Two Piece Doors

AC-1s of the 1st Aviation Company on the ramp at Fort Rucker, AL during July of 1962. True to its designation, the 1st was the first unit to use the Caribou operationally and the first unit to deploy with the Caribou to Southeast Asia. The lettering in the unit emblem on the tail states "WE SUPPORT." (U.S. Army)

An AC-1 of the 1st Aviation Company departs Fort Rucker during July of 1962. Propeller spinners were installed at the factory but were later deleted in the field by maintenance personnel during routine overhauls. (U.S. Army)

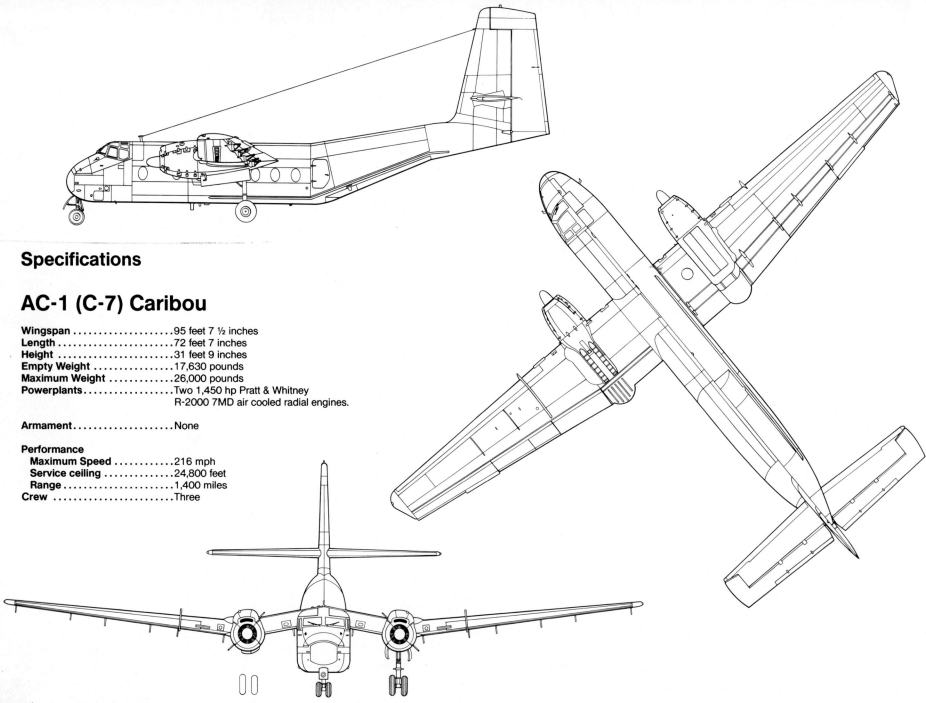

Specifications

AC-1 (C-7) Caribou

Wingspan	95 feet 7 ½ inches
Length	72 feet 7 inches
Height	31 feet 9 inches
Empty Weight	17,630 pounds
Maximum Weight	26,000 pounds
Powerplants	Two 1,450 hp Pratt & Whitney R-2000 7MD air cooled radial engines.
Armament	None

Performance

Maximum Speed	216 mph
Service ceiling	24,800 feet
Range	1,400 miles
Crew	Three

In a tradition normally used by the Air Force, this AC-1 (CV-2A) named *VAGABOND* on the ramp at Fort Eustis, VA in early 1966, carried two citations on the fuselage side below the cockpit. The propellers and spinners were in Natural Metal. (Terry Love)

Members of the 1st Aviation Company back a jeep up the boarding ramp of one of their AC-1 Caribous at Fort Rucker during May of 1962. The AC-1 Caribou could carry two jeeps in the cargo bay. (U.S. Army)

Four of the 1st Aviation Company's eighteen aircraft contingent enroute to Korat, Thailand during 1962. These were the first AC-1s to deploy to Southeast Asia. (U.S. Army)

AC-1A/CV-2B

To meet U.S. Department of Transportation requirements, the AC-1 was modified with a number of internal structural improvements to the airframe so that the Caribou could operate at a gross weight of 28,500 pounds. These changes were significant and the Army designated all Caribous produced after 11 July 1961 as AC-1As with deliveries of the new variant starting during 1963.

The increase in gross weight, while allowing the aircraft to carry a larger payload, had an adverse effect on performance. Takeoff distances, when fully loaded, rose to 725 feet (from 540 feet) and landing distances went up to 670 feet (from 525 feet). Takeoff distance to clear a 50 foot obstacle went to 1,185 feet (from 1,020). Before deliveries began, the Army redesignated the AC-1A to CV-2B.

The primary external difference between the CV-2A and CV-2B was the installation of an AN/APN-158 weather avoidance radar in a nose mounted radome. This radar installation was later retrofitted to early production CV-2Bs, most CV-2As and all five prototypes, making them externally identical. Another change was the deletion of the propeller spinner, although once again earlier aircraft were also modified making it difficult to distinguish one variant from another.

A bulk fuel delivery system was tested in one CV-2B during December of 1965 to meet an urgent Army requirement for long range operations in Vietnam. The system was comprised of three collapsible bulk fuel containers, each with a capacity of 350 gallons. Although it was seldom used, the system extended the CV-2B's range by 1,160 nautical miles. A similar system was fitted in a CV-2B by the 11th Air Assault Division (forerunner of the 1st Air Cavalry Division) to test the Caribou's capability as a tanker.

A total of 103 CV-2Bs were built and these were once again redesignated when they were transferred to the Air Force in 1966-67 as C-7A.

A fuel bladder, for delivery to a forward refueling site, is easily rolled off its trailer into the cargo compartment of an AC-1A Caribou during user tests held in 1965. This system was later adopted for use in Vietnam. (U.S. Army)

CV-2B were delivered from the factory in Gloss Olive Drab with high visibility markings, White Army on the nose and underwing and Yellow fin markings. This CV-2B was one of the initial production batch of CV-2Bs. (DeHavilland)

Support of twenty-eight Special Forces teams operating in Vietnam carried such a high priority that the Army formed a test Special Forces aviation unit at Fort Bragg, NC. This CV-2A was to be one of four assigned to the effort before Air Force opposition shelved the project. The SF emblem is visible behind the cockpit. (U.S. Army)

An early production CV-2B skims the ground as its cargo is pulled from the cabin by a parachute during a LOWLEX (low level extraction) run at Laguna Army Air Field, Yuma Proving Ground, AZ during 1964. (U.S. Army)

A parachute pulls a jeep from a the cargo bay of a low flying Caribou during a LOWLEX exercise held at Fort Gordon, Ga. This method of supply delivery would become very useful in Vietnam for delivering vital supplies to remote bases under fire. (U.S. Army)

Nose Development

AC-1/CV-2A

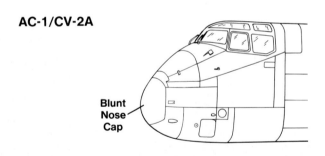

Blunt Nose Cap

AC-1A/CV-2B

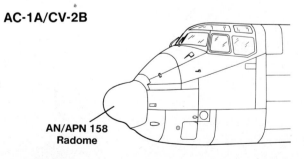

AN/APN 158 Radome

A CV-2B Caribou of the 61st Aviation Company undergoes a main landing gear strut change at a base in Thailand during August of 1965. This aircraft is an early production CV-2B without the radome for the weather avoidance radar. (Don Joyce)

The prominent upswept tail allowed easy access to the cargo compartment. This CV-2B (63-9759), parked with its nose in a hangar at Donaldson Air Force Base, SC during 1963, was one of the last CV-2Bs off the production line. (LTV via Pete Harlem)

Caribous were included in tests of the Army's airmobile concept during late 1964. This CV-2B of the 11th Air Assault Division (forerunner of the 1st Cav. Div.) was modified as a tanker. One of the tests involved refueling a Grumman OV-1A Mohawk of the 11th AAD. (U.S. Army)

Vietnam

As U.S. military involvement in Southeast Asia grew, the Caribou did not have to wait long for its baptism of fire. The CV-2 was considered as a candidate aircraft to increase the airlift capability of South Vietnamese forces during 1961 and in August of that year, a single aircraft was sent to Vietnam for combat tests. Originally flown from Danang, this Caribou operated under the auspices of the Advanced Research Projects Agency (ARPA) which had the authority to bypass bureaucratic "red tape" if the equipment and concepts being tested had an application for counterinsurgency (COIN) warfare. The ARPA Caribou was tested under field conditions into early 1962, flying into airfields in the A Shau Valley that were unable to handle the smaller U-6 Beaver or U-1 Otter.

In December of 1961, the Commander-In-Chief, Pacific (CINCPAC) rejected an Army proposal, based on the successful test deployment, to deploy a Caribou company to Vietnam. The reasons for this rejection centered around the fact that in-country fixed-wing transport requirements were already being met by USAF C-123s and an Army U-1 Otter company. Opposition to similar proposals continued until April of 1962 when Defense Secretary McNamara directed the Army to come up with fresh and if necessary, unorthodox concepts to greatly increase troop mobility in Vietnam.

Four months later the Airmobile concept was adopted and it included the Caribou for the forward air supply mission. The implementation of the Airmobile concept began a long standing feud between the Army and Air Force over tactical airlift responsibilities in Vietnam. Although the Air Force insisted that the C-123 could handle more than twice the Caribou's payload over three times the distance, the Provider required more runway for takeoff and proved less maneuverable for pinpoint cargo drops into confined areas, a task at which the Caribou excelled. The only serious drawback in the Caribou was its limited altitude capability which forced it to share lower flight levels with helicopter traffic and caused long course deviations to avoid artillery fire or bad weather.

At the insistence of the Military Assistance Command, Vietnam (MACV), Caribou deployment was approved in May of 1962, followed by the arrival of the eighteen aircraft of the 1st Aviation Company in Thailand during June of that year. The first CV-2 to serve operationally was the second aircraft off the production line (which went on to serve as the South Vietnamese presidential aircraft). Eight aircraft redeployed to Vietnam in July of 1963 for evaluation with the remaining ten aircraft being relocated to Vung Tau in December.

Despite Air Force opposition, the 61st Aviation Company deployed to Vung Tau in July with sixteen CV-2s and both units flew direct support missions throughout the country. Although the 1st Aviation Company was withdrawn from Vietnam in December of 1963 as part of a token troop reduction, a second Caribou company, the 92nd Aviation Company, returned in November of 1964 with sixteen aircraft, while a third unit, the 17th Aviation Company, arrived in September of 1965 and was based at Pleiku to support the 1st Air Cavalry Division at An Khe. One Caribou was converted into a flying command post by the Rollins Radio Company for use with the 1st Cav. Nine operator positions were installed along one side of the cabin to provide the commander with ready ground contact and long-range communications. The 57th, 134th and 135th Aviation Companies also deployed to Vietnam in December at GEN Westmoreland's request.

During 1963 the 1st Aviation Company CV-2s were modified with reversible pitch propellers, which greatly improved landing performance on wet surfaces and ground maneuverability. Caribous could now operate from some fifteen airfields which were previously rendered inoperable during the rainy season. These fields were still inadequate for C-123 operations. The addition of the nose mounted weather avoidance radar further increased the effectiveness of Vietnam-based Caribous; however, accidents remained a common occurrence, especially during short field landings and takeoffs.

Early in the war, Caribous were involved in frequent airdrops to Special Forces camps both by parachute and using free-fall methods. These missions became the Caribou's forte and crews also experimented with these methods for the resupply of forward patrols. Low Level Extraction (LOLEX) techniques proved more accurate than drops if the terrain permitted this method. The LOLEX system, evaluated from May to June of 1964 by the Aviation Test Board, used a parachute deployed behind the aircraft to pull palletized cargo (on rollers) out of the cargo compartment while the aircraft flew between three and fifteen feet off the ground. The Air Force later called this system LAPES (Low Altitude Parachute Extraction System) and did not encourage its use because of the possibility of a load hanging up or damaging the aircraft during delivery. Daily missions to Special Forces camps were high risk operations since crews had to make dangerous approaches and steep climbouts over enemy held territory surrounding these remote outposts. The Caribou's ability to outperform C-123 and C-130 aircraft in operating from these small airstrips was mainly due to its superior STOL handling characteristics. These characteristics prompted the Special Forces to request additional Caribou support during late 1964.

Designated A4s, Royal Australian Air Force Caribous (delivered in 1964) were sent directly to Vietnam where they formed the RAAF Caribou Flight at Vung Tau, flying under the call sign *Wallaby*. The RAAF flight remained in Vietnam for seven and a half years, becoming No 35 Squadron in 1966. Even though it had gained full squadron status, the unit was still better known by its nickname, *Wallaby Airlines*. Although the unit was incorporated into the centralized airlift system, it retained its primary mission — support of the Australian Task Force.

As Caribou use in combat increased, it was flown closer to its design limits. Numerous accounts are recorded describing Caribou operations with heavier than normal loads, flying into isolated mountain strips less than 1,000 feet long, or flying out of muddy strips so narrow that ground crewmen had to turn the aircraft around for the takeoff run. Caribous were instrumental in rushing fuel and cargo to forward areas during the major battle at Ia Drang during the Fall of 1965.

A Caribou touches down at the forward airstrip at Dak To in August of 1966. Missions to remote strips were usually high risk operations since security of the area often remained in question. (U.S. Army)

During January of 1967 the Air Force took over all Caribou operations in Vietnam from the Army, changing the aircraft designation to C-7. Although the operating agency changed, the missions flown by the Caribou crews did not. During 1968 and 1969, some 180,000 sorties were flown by USAF C-7 units.

As USAF units were phased out during early 1971, Caribous were gradually transferred to the South Vietnamese Air Force. The first VNAF unit, the 427th Transport Squadron (TS), was formed at Phu Cat, followed by a second unit, the 429th TS during mid-1972. A third unit, the 431st, was formed at Phu Cat and the 427th and 429th were transferred to Danang. During March of 1973, the 429th and 431st were relocated to Tan Son Nhut Air Base near Saigon. The last USAF unit in-country was the 457th TAS and was used to perform special airlift missions and train additional Vietnamese crews. Certain published accounts of the VNAF history list the 417th and 419th TS as being equipped with C-7s, although records are vague as to their operational dates and base locations.

Once the U.S. military left Vietnam during 1973, the VNAF found it impossible to maintain their C-7s. The aircraft suffered from engine problems, a lack of spare parts, corrosion and structural cracks. Most were put into storage at Pleiku, Danang and Tan Son Nhut with only about twenty percent of the force being maintained for training and short missions. During the communist takeover in 1975, six VNAF C-7s escaped to U-Tapao Air Base in Thailand while the remaining thirty-three fell into enemy hands.

A total of twenty U.S. Army/USAF Caribous were destroyed during the Vietnam conflict with a cost of thirty-one crewmen. Of a total of thirteen RAAF A4 Caribous in Vietnam, three were lost and four were damaged.

This Caribou was offloading spare helicopter rotor blades at a forward dirt strip in Vietnam during 1965 while a Medevac UH-1B Huey comes in for a landing. The aircraft was the first CV-2A built. (Smithsonian Institution)

GIZMOTCH was attached to the Blue Diamonds platoon of the 61st Aviation Company and carried that unit's insignia on the nose by the aircraft name. (Tom Hansen)

GIZMOTCH was a CV-2B of the 1st Flight Platoon, Blue Diamonds, 61st Aviation Company based at DaNang during late 1966. Aircraft of the 1st Flight Platoon carried a Blue diamond above the Y in the ARMY logo on the nose. (Tom Hansen)

Retrofitted with the radar nose, a CV-2B of the 61st Aviation Company takes off from a dirt strip in Vietnam during mid-1963. The 61st was the second Caribou unit to deploy to Vietnam. (U.S. Army)

With propellers still turning, a CV-2B of the 61st Aviation Company offloads supplies at a forward area base. As soon as the supplies were offloaded, the Caribou would make a quick takeoff since aircraft on the ground at a forward base would draw enemy fire. (U.S. Army)

SNAKE EATER 2 a CV-2A Caribou of the 61st Aviation Company, taxis out on the red dirt strip at Ban Me Thuot, Vietnam during 1963. The name was carried in White on the Flat Black anti-glare panel. (Al Adcock)

An oil splattered CV-2A of the 61st Aviation Company undergoes an engine change in the field with the aid of a plug-in boom hoist at Ban Me Thuot, Vietnam. The petal cowling was completely detached in order to to use the boom hoist, (Al Adcock)

Maintenance personnel inspect the new engine that will be installed on the CV-2A. The sidearms worn by ground and flight crewmen indicate that even engine changes on the Caribou were often performed under less than ideal conditions in Vietnam. (Al Adcock)

LONE WOLF was a CV-2B of the Red Diamonds Flight Platoon, 61st Aviation Company during late 1966. The aircraft carried a Red diamond on the nose gear door and next to the name. The engine nacelles and propeller are weathered from operations in rough terrain. (Tom Hansen)

Caribou Petal Cowling

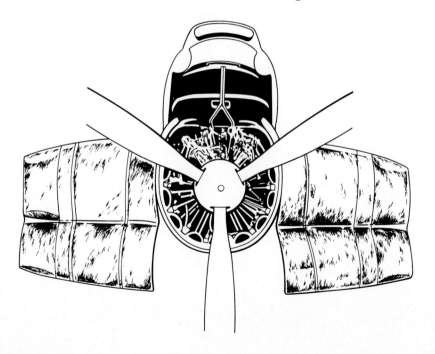

This CV-2B of the 57th Aviation Company "Gray Tiger Lines" carries the unit logo and a Tiger on the vertical fin in White. The 57th Aviation Company arrived in Vietnam during December of 1965. (Tom Hansen)

This CV-2 of the Red Diamonds Flight Platoon, 61st Aviation Company, carried a "Snoopy" character and the inscription *CURSE YOU BLUE DIAMOND*. The inscription referred to its rival, the Blue Diamond Flight Platoon of the same unit. (Tom Hansen)

Caribou missions in Vietnam's rough terrain were not without mishap, as evidenced by this CV-2A of the 61st Aviation Company which crashed on landing at Di Linh during 1963. (C. Blackman via Al Adcock)

This CV-2B of the 61st Aviation Company ran off the end of a crude strip during October of 1963. The retrofitting of reverse pitch propellers helped to reduce the number of such incidents. (C. Blackman via Al Adcock)

This CV-2A was destroyed on the ground by a direct hit from a Viet Cong mortar in South Vietnam. 61-2386 served with the 57th Aviation Company, the "Gray Tiger Lines," which deployed to Vietnam in December of 1965. (RAAF)

Several Caribous were flown by Air America in Southeast Asia including this early production model DHC-4 on the ramp at Danang during 1966. The aircraft has been retrofitted with a radar nose. (Tom Hansen)

N544Y was another Caribou operated by the Central Intelligence Agency's airline, Air America. The aircraft was an early production Caribou rated at 26,000 pounds gross weight.

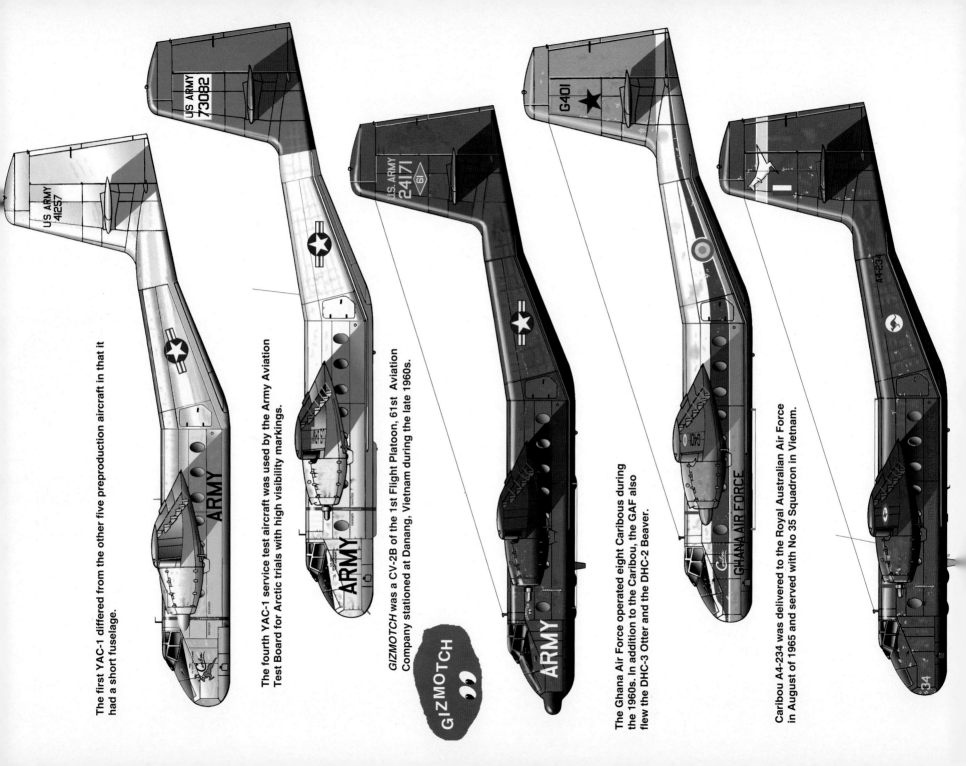

The first YAC-1 differed from the other five preproduction aircraft in that it had a short fuselage.

The fourth YAC-1 service test aircraft was used by the Army Aviation Test Board for Arctic trials with high visibility markings.

GIZMOTCH was a CV-2B of the 1st Flight Platoon, 61st Aviation Company stationed at Danang, Vietnam during the late 1960s.

GIZMOTCH

The Ghana Air Force operated eight Caribous during the 1960s. In addition to the Caribou, the GAF also flew the DHC-3 Otter and the DHC-2 Beaver.

Caribou A4-234 was delivered to the Royal Australian Air Force in August of 1965 and served with No 35 Squadron in Vietnam.

US ARMY 41257

US ARMY 73082

ARMY

ARMY

US ARMY 24171

ARMY

G401

GHANA AIR FORCE

A4-234

34

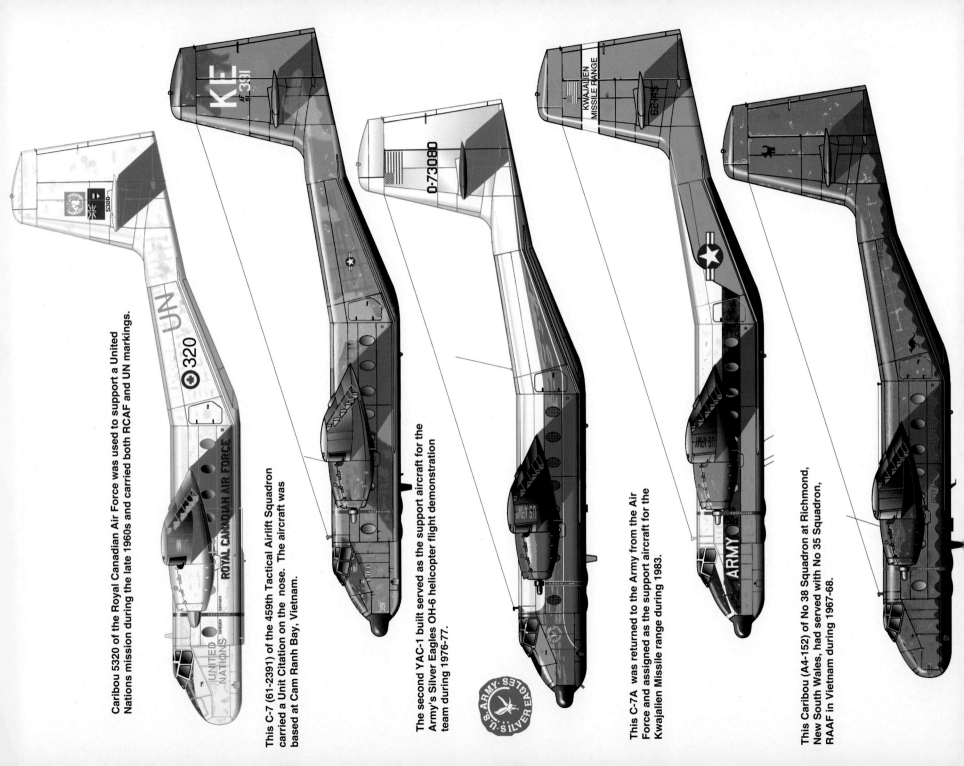

Caribou 5320 of the Royal Canadian Air Force was used to support a United Nations mission during the late 1960s and carried both RCAF and UN markings.

This C-7 (61-2391) of the 459th Tactical Airlift Squadron carried a Unit Citation on the nose. The aircraft was based at Cam Ranh Bay, Vietnam.

The second YAC-1 built served as the support aircraft for the Army's Silver Eagles OH-6 helicopter flight demonstration team during 1976-77.

This C-7A was returned to the Army from the Air Force and assigned as the support aircraft for the Kwajalien Missile range during 1983.

This Caribou (A4-152) of No 38 Squadron at Richmond, New South Wales, had served with No 35 Squadron, RAAF in Vietnam during 1967-68.

Pacific Architects & Engineers, Inc. was a subsidiary of Air America which operated two Caribous in Southeast Asia. N581PA was parked on the ramp at Cam Ranh Bay during 1971, painted in a White, Blue, and Gray color scheme. The aircraft was destroyed that same year while serving as a freight hauler in Alaska. (Tom Hansen)

This Caribou retained its C-7A designation after being passed back to the Army from the Air Force. It was assigned to the Army support unit at the Kwajalien Missile Range during 1983. The aircraft has been modified with a down opening fuselage boarding door with a built-in air stair. (Terry Love)

Fuselage Entry Door

This well maintained C-7 was one of nearly twenty Caribous in the Army inventory during the early 1980s. This aircraft, of the MO-Aviation Classification Repair Activity Depot, was one of a number returned to the Army by the Air Force when that service retired the Caribou. (Charles Stewart via Terry Love)

C-7 (Early)

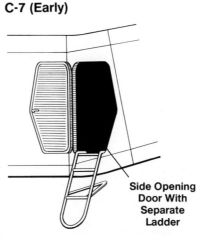

Side Opening Door With Separate Ladder

C-7 (Late)

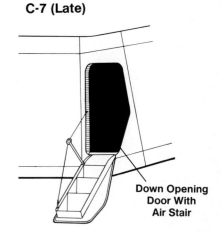

Down Opening Door With Air Stair

U.S. Air Force Caribou Operations

After a long and heated debate, the Army began transferring its Caribou and Buffalo aircraft to the Air Force during April of 1966. Part of the agreement was that the Army received blanket authority to develop all aspects of helicopter operations, including attack helicopter ground support operations. Called RED LEAF, the transfer of 144 CV-2s was completed by 31 December 1966. Fifteen aircraft were retained by the Army for administrative support duties. Prior to the changeover, the Tactical Air Command established the 4449th Combat Crew Training Squadron at Lawson Army Air Field, Fort Benning, GA. The squadron was equipped with sixteen aircraft and was tasked to provide training (by Army instructors) for USAF crews that were to man the Vietnam-based Caribou units.

The Air Force assigned the Caribou to the 56th Special Operations Wing (56th SOW) at Nakhon Phanom Air Base, Thailand and nine Tactical Airlift Squadrons (TAS) in Vietnam under the control of the 483rd Tactical Airlift Wing. Eight were located at Cam Ranh Bay and one was at Phu Cat. Each squadron had a strength of fourteen to sixteen aircraft.

Under Air Force control, the Caribous were redesignated as the C-7 and C-7A. Since most were stationed in Vietnam during the transition, the Caribou remained the logical choice for remote outpost support. Its reputation was partially gained through the use of highly experienced pilots recalled by the Air Force to fill new Caribou slots in Vietnam. Known as the "Grand Daddies" of the Caribou fleet, these pilots (more than fifty) were fighting in their third war.

The C-7s retained their Army Olive Drab camouflage schemes with USAF markings applied over the painted out Army markings. Eventually most were repainted in the Southeast Asian three tone camouflage typical of aircraft operating in Vietnam. Aircraft that had not already been retrofitted with the weather radar nose had the unit installed during rework.

During its first year in the Air Force inventory, the C-7 proved exceptionally effective in airlifts to forward combat areas, airdrops, extractions and casualty evacuation. During 1967, the Caribou force logged more than 100,000 combat hours. Among the many combat operations flown by Air Force Caribous was the siege at the Marine base of Khe Sanh. In late 1971 a number of C-7s were modified for communication relay work by installing additional radio gear and three operator positions in the cargo compartment. During the North Vietnamese Easter offensive of 1972 these aircraft flew twenty-four hour radio relay orbits flying out of Tan Son Nhut Air Base until mid-May.

This C-7 on the ramp at Cam Ranh Bay during 1971 was the first CV-2A off the assembly line. The aircraft was repainted in the three tone Southeast Asia camouflage and has the upper outboard wing panels painted in White to make the Caribou more visible to orbiting aircraft. (Tom Hansen)

An insight into USAF Caribou operations can be gained from the comments of Tom Hansen who exemplified the professionalism of USAF Caribou flight mechanics in Vietnam. With a wealth of experience in piston engined aircraft, Hansen was assigned to the 535th Tactical Air Support Squadron (TASS) Greentails which operated C-7s from Cam Ranh Bay during 1971 under the call sign *Tong*. Tom had previously served in Vietnam as an HU-16 Albatross flight mechanic with the 37th ARRS out of Danang during 1966-67. The 37th ARRS was the last active USAF squadron to use the Grumman amphibian.

The C-7 was a workhorse too, but of a different nature. It was an ugly duckling, a noisy crate, slow, did not have a great payload, but it was able to slow-fly almost like a Helio-Courier and get into and out of some ridiculous places mistakenly called airfields. It was a real bush aircraft! And simple, like the Beaver and Otter. Taking off empty, she would zoom-climb like you wouldn't believe until the airspeed bled off to a normal figure. I once saw, momentarily, 3,800 feet per minute climb.

The most exciting routine missions were hauling ammo into fire bases near the border since these hot areas ruled out the use of truck convoys. We hauled 105MM, 155MM, 175MM and eight inch howitzer projectiles into places such as Katum, Bu Dop, Djamap and Thien Ngon. Four or five birds flew these missions, flying four shuttles each from the hot loading ramp at Bien Hoa. We took one or two skids, depending on the projectile size, the maximum being about 4,200 pounds per skid. The 'grunts' unloaded each plane with a forklift if a usable one was available. More often than not the forklift was broke so we did a speed off-load by dumping the ammo out the back onto the ramp while the bird was moving. Although the grunts didn't like it that way, it was our fastest way to unload. When you're hauling 175s or eight inch "howies" into a place like Katum, minimum ground time is the name of the game.

Because it usually didn't work, the least desirable method to off-load was to have the grunts back a truck up to the back end of the bird. Then we were supposed to push the skid (two tons, mind you) off the plane onto the truck. Pushing a skid of shells in the aircraft was no problem — pushing it into the truck was! For most cargo sorties, the C-7 was configured with two cabin-length roller tracks enabling us to quickly load, unload, position a skid (a half-size C-130 type 463L pallet) or most importantly, jettison a load in case of engine failure. One man could move a skid load of up to two tons. We strapped down our loads in a manner that allowed us to remove all the tiedowns, except the last one in the event of a speed off-load at a hot fire base or emergency inflight jettison. The last strap was released or cut at the critical moment allowing the load to roll out. My squadron lost a plane on a single engine go-around at Dalat for lack of a good sheath knife when the flight mech undid the last strap and tossed it over the load. The load rolled aft as planned but hung up on the tail ramp when the tiedown ratchet snagged in the rollers. They couldn't climb single-engine with the center of gravity drastically out of limits so the Caribou "mushed" in two thirds of the way down the runway and slid down a hill. Luckily the crew escaped serious injury.

As we approached fire bases with an ammo load, the pilot flew the bird, watched for other traffic and ground fire while the copilot worked the radio, flaps and landing gear. The flight mech opened the rear cargo door and undid all the tie downs, except for the last one and ensured that nothing would foul the load. When the gear was on the ground, the props were reversed and the ramp trailed level with the floor. Meanwhile, the pilots changed trim and flap settings for takeoff. At the unloading area (usually located mid-field) we stopped with the nose pointed toward the active and reversed props, taxiing in reverse at five to ten knots while the flight mech undid the last strap. The pilots went to forward pitch to pull forward and the load slid to the rear. Being on

rollers it dumped out the back onto the ramp while we did a fast taxi to the runway with the copilot calling for clearance. When the approach end was clear we would scram. Total ground time from touchdown to liftoff was six to eight minutes.

The oddest cargo I ever carried (on three separate missions) consisted of 3,600 pounds of teletype paper (to an ARVN base I doubted had a teletype), one GI helmet strapped to a pallet and an ice-filled garbage can with three of the largest lobsters I've ever seen. It was a strange war.

As a part of the Vietnamization program, USAF units were deactivated during 1971 being replaced by three VNAF squadrons which began operations by late 1972. Aircraft not turned over to the VNAF were ferried back to the U.S. for rework and assignment to the Air Force Reserve. The 483rd Wing flew its last C-7 tactical mission on 25 March 1972; however, some aircraft were retained in-country and reassigned for special airlift work and training Vietnamese crews. Thirty-two C-7s that were ferried back to the U.S. went to the 94th Tactical Airlift Wing of the Air Force Reserve in the Spring of 1972.

The Air National Guard acquired a number of C-7s in June of 1973 and operated them until late 1980 when they were replaced by C-130s. Disposal of Air Force Reserve Caribous began in 1980 with a large number being transferred to the Spanish Air Force during 1981-82. The last USAF Caribous served with the Reserve 357th TAS at Maxwell AFB being replaced by C-130s in October of 1983. Some examples were given back to the Army which had nineteen in the inventory as late as 1986.

The Caribou obviously left its mark as evidenced by statements made by military officials in 1984 citing a serious void in intratheatre airlift since the "feeder" C-7 aircraft were never replaced.

This Air Force C-7 in flight over Vietnam during June of 1967 retained its original Army Olive Drab camouflage. The aircraft was converted into an airborne radio relay station with numerous radio antennas protruding from the rear cargo bay. (USAF)

This C-7A and its crew were lost in August of 1967 while on a supply mission to Ha Thann in I Corps area. The 459th TAS Caribou was on approach when it was hit by an outgoing 155MM shell from a U.S. artillery battery located on the airstrip perimeter. A ceasefire order had been given to allow the aircraft to land but was never received by the battery. (Via Ron Verner)

Supplies are quickly unloaded from a C-7A of the 459th TAS on the muddy field at Tra Bong during February of 1970. It was common practice to keep the engines running during off loading since a Caribou at a forward area presented an inviting target for enemy gunners. (USAF)

Air Force personnel inspect the wreckage of an early production Air Force C-7 (61-2399). Explosives hidden and later detonated by a North Vietnamese sapper totally destroyed the aircraft on the ramp at Vung Tau during 1967. (U. Castells via Pete Harlem)

A "Bou" crew of the 535th Tactical Airlift Squadron, based at Cam Ranh Bay, poses with their C-7 prior to their last mission in 1971. Flight mechanic Tom Hansen is at left along with the aircraft commander (AC) and copilot. (Tom Hansen)

This Air Force C-7 Caribou on final approach to Cam Ranh Bay during early 1967 carries no unit insignia. The aircraft is fresh from rework and carries the Southeast Asia camouflage. (Tom Hansen)

Not all Caribous were repainted in the tri-tone camouflage when turned over to the Air Force. This C-7 of the 537th Tactical Airlift Squadron at Phu Cat Air Base in October of 1970 retained the Army overall Olive Drab scheme. (Norm Taylor)

Freshly remarked Caribous on the ramp at Tan Son Nhut AB during early 1967. Maintenance was often performed "in the weather" with the aid of roofed engine work stands. Low altitude limitations prompted Army crews to paint the fuselage spines White to make them more visible to aircraft at higher altitudes. (Bob Chenoweth)

An Air Force C-7 undergoes routine engine maintenance on the ramp at Cam Ranh Bay during 1971 with the aid of a fork lift. The "petal" cowling on the C-7 gave maintenance crews excellent access to the engine. (Tom Hansen)

The 535th Tactical Airlift Squadron was based at Cam Ranh Bay during 1967 and operated a mix of Southeast Asia camouflaged and overall Olive Drab C-7 Caribous. The unit carried the tail code KH on the fin in White. (Bob Chenoweth)

Caribous of the 458th Tactical Airlift Squadron at Cam Ranh Bay were identified by their Red fin tips. This C-7A on the ramp at Cam Ranh Bay during 1971 has the undersurfaces painted Black for night supply missions. (Tom Hansen)

This C-7 in flight over the South Vietnamese coast carries a unit citation award badge painted on the nose and a White fin tip. The White fin tip identified the aircraft as belonging to the 459th TAS based at Cam Ranh Bay. (USAF)

This flight of Air Force C-7 Caribous on their return trip to the U.S. during 1971 have had their Vietnam squadron tail codes painted out. The USAF C-7 squadrons had been replaced in Vietnam by Vietnamese Air Force (VNAF) units. (Tom Hansen)

Antenna Configuration

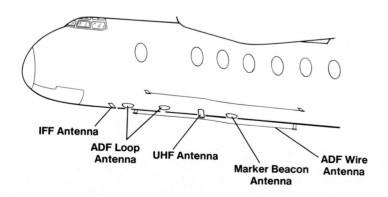

IFF Antenna

ADF Loop
Antenna   UHF Antenna

Marker Beacon
Antenna

ADF Wire
Antenna

A C-7 of the 700th Tactical Airlift Squadron, 94th Tactical Airlift Wing, Air Force Reserve on the ramp at Dobbins Air Force Base, GA during early 1980. C-7s assigned to Reserve units carried the Blue and Yellow reserve band on the fin with the legend AFRES in White. (Werner Hartman via Terry Love)

The last USAF unit to use the Caribou was the 357th TAS, 94th TAW Air Force Reserve based at Maxwell AFB, Al. The aircraft carried an unusual paint scheme in that it had a Black demarcation pattern on the fuselage and engine nacelles. The Black areas were probably retained from a wartime Black underside scheme which was later painted out. (Terry Love)

Some Air National Guard units operated Caribous from 1973 to 1980 when they were replaced by Lockheed C-130s. This weathered C-7 served the 150th Tactical Airlift Squadron of the New Jersey Air National Guard. (Hugh Muir via Terry Love)

This refurbished C-7A was transferred from the Air Force to the 20th Special Forces Group, Alabama Army National Guard during the mid-1980s. Army National Guard units carried the state two letter code and ARNG on the fin in Black. (Norm Taylor)

A number of C-7s Caribous were sealed and placed in storage at Davis-Monthan Air Force Base during late 1979. Some of these aircraft were later withdrawn from storage and sold to friendly foreign governments. (Terry Love)

This Alabama Army National Guard C-7, chocked and tied down on the ramp at Montomery Army National Guard base, has the Army National Guard insignia on the nose near the aircraft side number and the legend U.S. Army on the fuselage side in Black. (Norm Taylor)

35

In Foreign Service

Canada

When Canada's Chief of Staff learned of the U.S. Army interest in the Caribou design, he ordered his command to conduct a number of studies of the aircraft and pledged to support the project with funding. A total of nine aircraft were delivered to the Royal Canadian Air Force (RCAF) including the first prototype, which was delivered on 22 July 1960. Continued development of the prototype was accomplished with the full cooperation of the Canadian Department of Defense.

During late-1960, the RCAF took delivery of three more Caribous. These first five aircraft were designated CC-108-1As, while the remaining four aircraft delivered in 1964 were designated CC-108-1Bs with the last example being taken on strength on 20 September 1964.

Their first assignment came in the Fall of 1960 when three Caribous were sent to Egypt for duty with the U.N. peace keeping force. Throughout the 1960s, Canadian Caribous were kept busy with similar tasks in Yemen, Cyprus, India and Pakistan, while Search and Rescue became the primary role for those remaining in Canada. Five Caribous spent several weeks in Peru during mid-1970 flying relief missions following a devastating earthquake. Finally, during 1971, the RCAF sold eight of the nine aircraft to the Tanzanian government.

Australia

To replace their fleet of aging Douglas Dakotas (C-47s), the Royal Australian Air Force (RAAF) ordered eighteen Caribous, the first of which was delivered on 25 February 1964, with the remaining seventeen delivered throughout the remainder of that year. Designated A-4s, additional orders followed and a total of thirty-three Caribous were eventually delivered to the RAAF.

The first Caribous delivered were sent directly to Vietnam where they formed the Caribou Flight based at Vung Tau. Reinforced and renamed No 35 Squadron in 1966, the unit became better known by its nickname *Wallaby Airlines* (the name came from the unit's call sign *Wallaby*). During their seven and a half year stay in Vietnam, *Wallaby Airlines* carried some 600,000 passengers, lost three of its thirteen aircraft in combat and had another four damaged.

After returning from Vietnam, the remaining RAAF Caribous were split between No 35 Squadron and No 38 Squadron which operated a flight of A-4s from Port Moresby, Papua New Guinea for several years. This flight provided airlift support for the newly formed Papua New Guinea Defense Force (PNGDF) until the PNGDF acquired transports of their own. Another Caribou was deployed out of country on assignment with the U.N. forces in India-Pakistan from April 1975 to December 1978.

Assigned as part of the Tactical Transport Wing, both units operated their Caribous from Richmond Air Base in New South Wales. At one point, the RAAF considered re-engining its Caribous with turboprop engines; however, the technical problems associated with replacing 4,000 pound radials engines with 1,200 pound turbo-props made the project impractical.

This early production DHC-4 Caribou carries a civil registration for its factory test flight. The aircraft was one of nine DHC-4 and DHC-4A aircraft delivered to the Canadian government. (DeHavilland via Al Drake)

India

The government of India was one of the larger Caribou customers operating nineteen aircraft. In January of 1963, two U.S. Army Caribous were loaned to the Indian Air Force for an evaluation program of aircraft operations in mountainous terrain.

Other Operators

The C-7 was flown by seventeen countries including: Spain (twelve aircraft designated T-9s which were retired during late 1992), Tanzania (twelve), Ghana (eight), Zambia (seven), Kenya (six), United Arab Emirates (four), Cameroon (two), Zaire (two), Iran (one) and Kuwait (two). Uganda ordered one for their Police Air Wing and three went to the Royal Thai Police Force. U.S. forces in Vietnam eventually passed nearly fifty C-7s to the Vietnamese Air Force (VNAF), most of which fell into North Vietnamese hands when the country fell in 1975. The Royal Malaysian Air Force operates a total of seventeen C-7s, including the last Caribou built, which was delivered to the RMAF during 1973.

Civil Caribous

Many Caribous served civil aviation over the years in a variety of roles. Once commercial operators realized the aircraft's ruggedness, maneuverability and ability to operate in isolated areas with rough terrain and severe climates, orders for the DHC-4 civil variant began to come in. These aircraft were used for "brush airlines," freight hauling, mining exploration, logging work, research and many more uses. Freight carriers found that loading through the Caribou's tail cargo ramp facilitated quick bulk container transfer enabling fast turnarounds and higher profits. Civil passenger versions could accommodate some thirty passengers in the cargo compartment.

The first civil operator of the Caribou was Nordair who leased the second prototype (CF-LAN) from DeHavilland in 1961 to fulfill a cargo transport contract in sub-arctic climates. This operation was the first use of the DHC-4 in sub-arctic operations and was closely monitored by DeHavilland officials.

In the mid-1960s, Imperial Oil and American Petroleum used Caribous to transport seismic and drilling crews into short dirt strips in Northwestern Alberta, Canada. Two Caribous were used by Civil Air Transport in Taiwan before being turned over to Air America for service in Southeast Asia during the 1960s. Air America, the unofficial air arm of the Central Intelligence Agency (CIA), was known to have operated at least four DHC-4s in Southeast Asia (SEA) during the mid-1960s. One of these aircraft was modified in Singapore to increase its seating capacity to carry some forty-four passengers. Pacific Architects and Engineers, a subsidiary of Air America, operated two Caribous in SEA for similar tasks. It was reported that four machines ordered for Air Asia of Taiwan were also used for covert operations in SEA.

Global Associates of California operated three Caribous on a lease-purchase agreement with DeHavilland to support the Nike-X test site in the Kwajalien Missile Range located in the Marshall Islands. These aircraft were transferred to the U.S. government during mid-1970. SEAAIR used two aircraft on Alaskan freight routes during the 1970s and Aerolineas Condor of Ecuador operated a number of second-hand Caribous in the rugged Andes Mountains well into the 1980s. Union Flights of California operated six ex-U.S. military Caribous and several have appeared on the Civil Aircraft Register in Canada.

Some of the last civil Caribous built were purchased by Guyana Airways for use on their domestic routes. Three aircraft formerly operated by Propair of Quebec were sold to a Panamanian dealer for use in El Salvador. These aircraft were reportedly involved with supplying Nicaraguan Contra rebels.

Most Caribous employed by civil operators were ex-military aircraft, although twenty-two were purchased directly from DeHavilland. Some have changed hands many times before being retired while others continue to serve under civil registry.

This Royal Canadian Air Force DHC-4A carries the overall White scheme used by aircraft assigned to United Nations duty. The aircraft carries the Blue UN insignia on the fin and the United Nations logo on the fuselage side.

A4-185 was one of the first RAAF Caribous diverted to Vietnam and was the first RAAF aircraft to receive battle damage (12 November 1964). Six days later, a failed air drop prompted the pilot to land with the urgently needed supplies at A Ro and the aircraft crashed landed. (via Chas. Van Hulsentop)

The fuselage of this crashed RAAF Caribou was turned into an observation bunker at A Ro and named "Hammond House," after the pilot. Later the fuselage was eventually dug out and put to use as a parachute training platform. (RAAF via Chas. Van Hulsentop)

This RAAF Caribou (A4-202) crashed on a fuel delivery flight to Pogera Airstrip, Papua New Guinea on 3 June 1965, when it overshot an attempted landing on an uphill slope. (RAAF via Chas. Van Hulsentop)

Just ten weeks after the Royal Australian Air Force took delivery of Caribou A4-134, it was destroyed in a landing accident at Nowra NSW on 1 July 1964. The fuselage went to the Army Transportation Museum at Albury New South Wales. (RAAF)

This RAAF Caribou (A4-264) crashed at Camden New South Wales during July of 1986 when it drifted off the runway centerline before touchdown. One propeller was ripped from its shaft and thrown far in front of the aircraft. (Chas. Van Hulsentop)

Demonstrating the Caribou's wide performance range, Squadron Leader Harrison of No 38 Squadron, RAAF does a nosewheel first landing in Caribou A4-164 during an airshow held in August of 1987. (via Chas. Van Hulsentop)

Eight Caribous of No 38 Squadron, Royal Australian Air Force taxi out in formation at Richmond during the 1980s. The crew chief of each aircraft is riding in the open upper fuselage escape hatch. (via Chas. Van Hulsentop)

Australian Caribous have also seen service with the United Nations. This Caribou (A4-199) carries Australian national insignia on its overall White United Nations paint scheme while in Australia between tours of duty with UN observer forces. (RAAF)

While Caribous were known for their tenacity in hot climates, they performed equally well in cold climates. This RAAF Caribou (A4-235) is flying over the snow covered mountains of Tasmania. (via Chas. Van Hulsentop)

Caribous of No 38 Squadron Royal Australian Air Force fly a tight trail formation. Normally RAAF Caribous operate singlely or in pairs and detachments are based at a number of locations throughout Australia. (via Chas. Van Hulsentop)

RAAF Caribou A4-173 suffered two serious accidents in Vietnam, one in May of 1965 and the other on 16 August 1966. The August 1966 accident took place at the Ba To Special Forces camp where it landed short. After ten days of temporary repairs, the Caribou was flown out and continues to serve with the RAAF. (RAAF via Chas. Van Hulsentop)

A4-140 was the RAAF's oldest surviving Caribou. It had been delivered with the first batch during April of 1964 and had seen combat in Vietnam. The Red Cross markings were applied for relief flights to Timoor during 1975. (via Chas. Van Hulsentop)

This No 38 Squadron Caribou (A4-208) was painted in a Tan, Red-Brown and Black wrap-around camouflage for camouflage trials held during 1987. The Kangaroo marking on the fuselage and number on the nose were in Black. (Chas. Van Hulsentop)

Assigned to No 38 Squadron, RAAF, this Caribou (A4-164) carries the current RAAF camouflage of Green, Black and Tan. The RAAF insignia on the fuselage has been reduced to a small Kangaroo in Gray and the serial is carried in Tan. (Chas. Van Hulsentop)

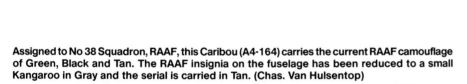

This Caribou began life as the third CV-2A off the production line. It saw duty in Vietnam, served with the 700th TAS, 94th TAW at Dobbins AFB, GA and then was sold to Spain. The aircraft awaits delivery to the Spanish Air Force during October of 1981 with the USAF markings over painted in dark Gray. (R. Leader via Pete Harlem)

These DHC-4s (believed to be ex-Kenyan or ex-Zambian Air Force) await overhaul and repainting in Malta during 1988 prior to onward shipment to the U.S. The aircraft were purchased by Newcal Aviation, a private low profile company. (Mike Terrel)

This DHC-4 was one of seventeen aircraft assigned to two squadrons of the Royal Malaysian Air Force. RMAF Caribous were finished in an overall Flat Olive Drab. The last Caribou built went to the RMAF and this aircraft, on the ramp in Singapore during early 1967, was fitted with a fold-down air stair passenger door on the port side. (via Norm Taylor)

This DHC-4 Caribou on the ramp at Edinburgh, Scotland in January of 1972 was one of two Caribous delivered to the Kuwaiti Army. The aircraft carried both English and Arabic lettering and numbers. (via Al Adcock)

This DHC-4 was purchased by the Uganda Police Force in January of 1966. It was finished in overall Off-White with Dark Blue trim. The aircraft crashed in May of 1976 and was totally destroyed. (DeHavilland)

This DHC-4 was one of three Caribous flown by the Sultan of Oman Air Force. Oman flew the Caribou for only a short period of time, replacing them with Short Skyvan transports. (via Terry Love)

DHC-5/C-8 Buffalo

The 1960s trend toward turbine-powered military aircraft inevitably led to discussions for a larger turbine-powered derivative of the Caribou. U.S. Army leaders speculated that the heavy demand for Caribous in Vietnam would prove the need for an advanced version and subsequently pave the way for Army participation in the follow-on program. In the Spring of 1962 DeHavilland won a U.S. Army competition for a STOL aircraft capable of carrying the same tactical loads as the Boeing Vertol CH-47 Chinook helicopter (which was just entering production). Originally called the Caribou II, DeHavilland renamed the aircraft the DHC-5 Buffalo and the Army gave the aircraft the designation AC-2 (which became CV-7A in 1962).

Prototype development was undertaken as a cost sharing agreement between the company and the U.S. and Canadian governments. The first stage in the development program consisted of outfitting the first prototype Caribou airframe with two 2,850 hp GE YT-64-GE-4 turboprop engines as a flying test bed. This aircraft made its first flight on 22 September 1961 and was flown for some 300 hours. In March of 1963, the U.S. Army awarded DeHavilland a contract for four prototypes; however, further Buffalo development was not without its setbacks. Since the Canadian design had won out over entries from U.S. companies, pressure from these companies forced changes in U.S. military procurement policies designed to protect U.S. industry. This change in policy limited sales to the U.S. Army to the four CV-7A evaluation aircraft (63-13686 to 689), which were delivered in the Spring of 1965.

Development of the DHC-5 slowed while other customers were sought. The first customer was the RCAF which ordered fifteen Buffalos under the designation CC-115. Other early orders came from Brazil and Peru while later customers included: India, Zaire, Zambia and Ecuador. During late 1965 the U.S. Army proposed the procurement of 120 Buffalos, a proposal that the U.S. Air Force viewed as an expensive duplication of the Fairchild C-123 Provider. Secretary of Defense McNamara settled the dispute by ruling out any further procurement of the Buffalo in December of 1965.

The Buffalo was a more sophisticated version of the Caribou with increased overall dimensions, having a maximum payload of 41,000 pounds. Except for its distinctive "T" tail which cleared the airflow behind the high-lift flaps and turboprop engines, the Buffalo retained the basic Caribou profile. This reduced the need for new tooling and cut development costs. The wing span was 96 feet, length was 77 feet 3 inches, and the height was 28 feet 7 inches. The DHC-5 made its first flight in April of 1964, and, like its "little brother," proved its STOL capability by landing within 1,050 feet and taking off within 1,225 feet (at gross weight over a 50 foot obstacle). The Buffalo could lift forty-one troops or up to twenty-five litter patients. It had an empty weight of 22,486 pounds, a top speed of 267 mph at sea level, a cruising speed (at 5,000 feet) of 277 mph and a range of 530 miles.

The Army-Air Force controversy over the Caribou mission and ownership carried over to the Buffalo program prompting the Department of Defense to transfer the four CV-7As Buffalos to the Air Force as part of the Caribou transfer. In the interim, two Buffalos were sent to Vietnam for a three month evaluation beginning in November of 1965. These were assigned to the 92nd Aviation Company at Nha Trang and used primarily to support the 5th Special Forces Group. Since these aircraft were still in the research and development stage at the time of their transfer to the USAF, they were assigned to the Air Force Systems Command for tests on 1 July 1966 under the designation C-8A. During the 1970s all four examples were passed on to other U.S. Government agencies.

DeHavilland's Buffalo logo is carried on the nose of this Canadian C-8B. This Buffalo was powered by a pair of 2,580 shp GE T-64-820-1 turboprop engines. Like the C-7A, the C-8 carried a weather radar in a nose mounted radome. (DeHavilland via Al Drake)

In post-war discussions concerning USAF commitments to Army airlift support, the Air Force sought additional Caribous, or as a possible alternative, the Buffalo. Other aircraft considered included a turboprop variant of the C-123 and a C-130 variant modified for short-field work. The DHC-5 production program was shelved temporarily during early 1972 after fifty-nine aircraft had been delivered to foreign customers. Increased engine power from the T-64 led to an improved DHC-5D model and Buffalo production resumed in 1974. The original DHC-5 had been designed to fill the STOL tactical role, while the DHC-5D was intended to carry larger payloads on conventional missions operating from hard surfaced runways.

Climb tests with a standard production Buffalo led to six new time-to-height world records being set on 23 February 1976. Buffalos were also employed for a number of experimental programs. One had an original Canadian CC-115 redesignated as the XC-8A and modified to test the Bell Air Cushion Landing System (ACLS) during 1972. Another C-8A was modified for the Augmentor Wing Jet STOL project which was being developed jointly through NASA and the Canadian government. The project involved augmenting normal wing lift by ducting turbofan engine air to a trailing edge slot.

A program launched by Boeing, under NASA, during 1976 created a short-haul research Buffalo variant which utilized four turbofan engines which exhausted over and through the wings. This greatly enhanced performance and control at low speeds.

Production of the Buffalo ended in December of 1986 after some 126 aircraft had been delivered.

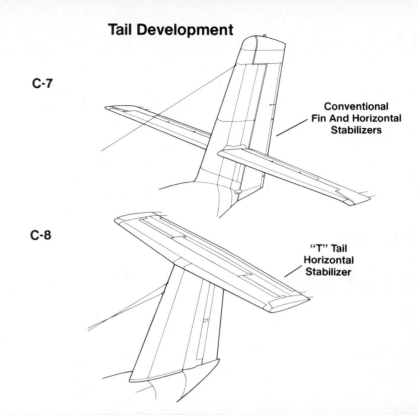

Tail Development

C-7 — Conventional Fin And Horizontal Stabilizers

C-8 — "T" Tail Horizontal Stabilizer

Canadian Armed Forces Buffalos were used for search and rescue duties. The aircraft are painted overall Yellow with Black and Red trim. This aircraft side number on the nose and under the wing consists of the last three digits of the aircraft serial (carried on the fin). (DeHavilland via Al Drake)

45

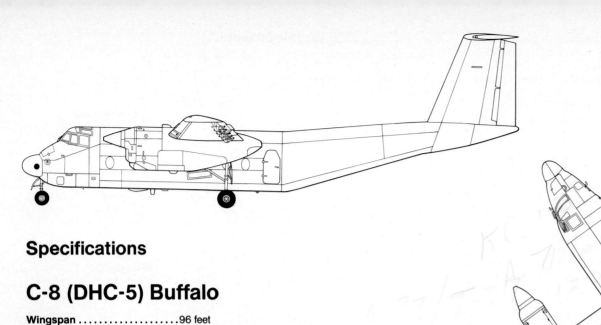

Specifications

C-8 (DHC-5) Buffalo

Wingspan .96 feet
Length . . . . .77 feet 3 inches
Height .28 feet 7 inches
Empty Weight . . . . .22,486 pounds
Maximum Weight . . . . .41,000 pounds
Powerplant . . . . .Two 2,850 shp General Electric
T-64 turboprop engines.

Armament . . . . .None

Performance
  Maximum Speed . . . . .277 mph
  Service ceiling . . . . .25,000 feet
  Range . . . . .530 miles
Crew . . . . .Three

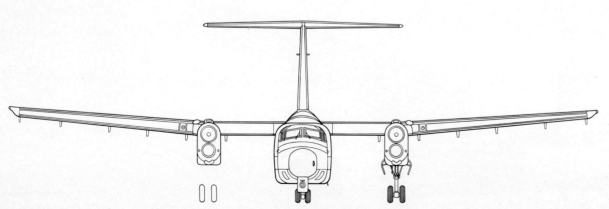

When turned over to the Air force as part of the Caribou transfer, the four CV-7A Buffalos were redesignated C-8As. The first aircraft retained the Olive Drab finish with the Air Force Systems Command (AFSC) patch on the nose. (Smithsonian Institution)

Engine Development

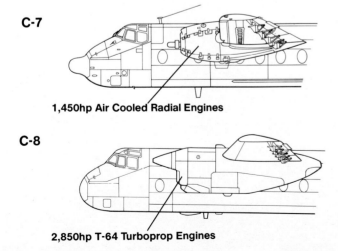

C-7

1,450hp Air Cooled Radial Engines

C-8

2,850hp T-64 Turboprop Engines

Bearing a strong family resemblance to the basic Caribou, the second YCV-7A Buffalo makes an evaluation flight. The aircraft was finished in standard Army overall Olive Drab and full Army markings. The probe on the port wingtip was an instrument test probe. (DeHavilland)

47

The XC-8A takes off from Wright Patterson Air Force Base, Dayton, Ohio on a cushion of air. Combination outriggers and floats were fitted on the wingtips so that the aircraft could be operated from either ground or water. (via Al Adcock)

The belly mounted air cushion was fed by the large duct running along the fuselage side from the air compressors mounted under the wing root. To signify the joint test program, the aircraft carried both USAF and Canadian Forces insignia. (Bell-Textron via Al Adcock)

This C-115 Buffalo was modified during 1972 to test the Air Cushion Landing System (ACLS) under a joint Canadian/U.S. effort. The Buffalo was redesignated the XC-8A and was used to test the feasibility using a large belly-mounted cushion filled with air from side-mounted compressors for ground operations. (Bell-Textron via Al Adcock)

A Peruvian Air Force Buffalo (FAP 322) undergoes an engine change on the ramp at its home base. The tail is supported by a jack stand to keep the aircraft from sitting on its tail. (via N.J. Waters III)

Brazil operated twenty-four Bufflaos, assigning them to the 5th and 6th Transport Squadrons of the 1st Transport Group. The Buffalos are tasked with direct support of Army operations.

USAF In Vietnam

1047

1060

1065

1114

1118

1120

1124

1130

 **squadron/signal publications**

This A4 Caribou of No 38 Squadron, Royal Australian Air Force was painted in this camouflage for a camouflage test during the mid-1980s. A4-208 was the only RAAF A4 to carry this scheme.

Members of the Army's Golden Knights parachute team exit their jump aircraft, the last YAC-1 Caribou built, during the mid-1980s. There were several different color schemes used on this aircraft during its career with the team.

ISBN 0-89747-292